Life of Pi

by Yann Martel

A Study Guide by Ray Moore

Acknowledgements:

Thanks, as always, are due to Barbara for reading the manuscript and making many helpful suggestions, and for putting the text into the correct formats for publication. Any errors which remain are my own.

I am indebted to the work of numerous translators, biographers, and critics as I have acknowledged in the Bibliography. As always, I am very aware that I stand on the shoulders of giants. Where I am conscious of having taken an idea, or actual words, from a particular author, I have cited the source in the text. Any failure to do so is an omission which I will immediately correct if it is drawn to my attention.

Where I have selectively quoted from the writings of others in the course of my own argument, I have done so in the sincere belief that this constitutes fair use.

Contents

Genre

The novel is fundamentally a classic *bildungsroman*, that is, a Coming of Age story in which the reader watches Pi struggle towards a real understanding of himself and his relationship to the world.

Life of Pi is a work of *magical realism*, a literary *genre* in which fantastical elements – such as animals with human personalities or an island with cannibalistic trees – appear in an otherwise realistic setting. It is also an adventure story in the tradition of *Robinson Crusoe*.

Life of Pi contains elements of nonfiction *genre*s such as *autobiography* and *journalism* (Martel claims to have heard the story of Pi while backpacking through Pondicherry. At the end of the novel, the author includes *interview transcripts*, another *genre* of nonfiction writing.

Themes

1. Belief:

The novel poses the question: Where does man go in understanding existence once the limits of reason are reached? The answer that Pi offers is to take a leap of faith in God. Writing a theological novel is really unusual and high-risk. Pi's assertion of the syncretism, or union, of the principals of the three major religions to which he is exposed is illustrated by his conviction that, in order to know God, he must be a Hindu, Muslim and Christian at the same time challenges orthodox teaching in these religions; think of Christian/Muslim conflicts such as the Crusades and Hindu/ Muslim conflicts such as the Gujarat riots (1969) and the Bhagalpur riots (1989) in India. Not surprisingly, some have criticized the presentation of religious belief in the novel as "inconsistent, or overly simplistic," whilst others have praised it (GradeSaver).

2. Science and Religion:

Largely because of his life-experiences, Pi's first degree involves the unusual pairing of religious studies and biology. Science and religion are frequently seen as in opposition, but the novel argues that there is no conflict: science, a branch of reason, helps us to understand and control the world; however, science only takes us so far. After that, it takes faith to understand existence. Martel has said, "Rationality is only part of the picture. Science and religion don't have to collide - I see them as complementary, rather than contradictory. Science can be a gateway to the greater mystery" (Renton).

3. Telling a Story:

This is a novel with multiple *narrators* (the author, Mr. Francis Adirubasamy, Pi, Mr. Okamoto and Mr. Chiba). Every teller brings his own bias to the story. As Pi says, "'Isn't just looking upon this world already something of an invention? ... The world isn't just the way it is. It is how we understand it, no?'" (302). This, of course, raises the question: How does the reader know what to believe? For example, exactly how much of the author's frame story can the reader believe? Pi suggests that we should not ask which of two stories is the more realistic but which is "'the better story'" (317). Martel stated his own conclusions thus, "1) Life is a story. 2) You can choose your story. 3) A story with God is the better story" (Renton).

4. Freedom:

The novel shows repeatedly that in both the animal and human world freedom is not an absolute value. Animals and people actually accept limits because they are more comfortable in a world which they understand. *Ironically*, Pi is most free when surrounded by the limitless Pacific Ocean, but that freedom is meaningless. Every creature needs its own territory: humans call that territory 'home.' Every creature creates rituals, habits, and schedules because they feel more comfortable within these self-imposed confines.

5. Survival:

The novel contains many examples from the animal and human world of adaptation to survive. In the face of death, Pi has to abandon some of his most cherished beliefs, most notably his vegetarianism. Some of the things that both animals and people do in the novel in order to survive are heroic, but others are horrific.

6. Coming of Age:

The whole story of survival can be seen as a symbol for Pi's passage to adulthood. He loses his parents and is literally on his own.

The Title of the Novel

Significantly, Pi's name combines the finite and the infinite. His full name, Piscine Molitor Patel, is inspired by a Parisian swimming pool used for the 1924 Paris Olympics. Thus the pool is carefully measured to conform to regulations, but Mamaji also calls it "'a pool the gods would have delighted to swim in'" (11). The shortened form, Pi, is the ratio of a circle's circumference divided by its diameter, the number 3.1415926..., an irrational number that goes on forever without discernible pattern.

About the title, Martel has said, "Like 'pi', life is not finite. And so I didn't make the title *The Life of Pi*: I deliberately left out the definite article. That would have denoted a single life. This book is not escapist fiction. It's to do with discovering life through a religious perspective" (Renton).

Dramatis personae

The Author supplies a few comments throughout the novel to place Pi's story in context. His contributions are the italicized chapters. This character is a fictionalized version of Yann Martel (both live in Canada, have published two books, and were inspired to write Pi's life story while visiting India). The effect is to give the narrative a feeling of realism.

Francis Adirubasamy (Marmaji) meets the author in a Pondicherry coffee shop, tells him of Pi's remarkable adventure and arranges for the author to meet Pi. He is a friend of the Patel family and a former Olympic swimmer who taught Pi to swim as a child. *Mamaji* is an Indian term that means 'respected uncle.'

The Patel Family:

Piscine Molitor Patel (Pi) is the narrator and protagonist of the story which centers on his experience of surviving for 227 days in a lifeboat in the Pacific Ocean which he shared with a 450 pound Bengal tiger. He does not come from a religious family, but finds himself fascinated by attempts to reconcile the teachings is Hinduism, Islam and Christianity.

Santosh Patel is Pi's father and the manager of the Pondicherry Zoo. In this capacity, he teaches his sons how to care for and control wild animals, but also how important it is to respect the danger that they pose. It is his decision to emigrate with his family to Canada that leads to Pi's remarkable adventure.

Gita Patel is Pi's mother and protector. She encourages Pi's love of reading.

Auntie Rohin is Pi's mother's elder sister. She is one of the few members of the family who remains traditionally religious and takes Pi to a Hindu temple as a baby.

Ravi is Pi's older brother. In character they are very different, Ravi having none of Pi's interest in religions.

Auntieji is Pi's foster mother when he finally gets to Toronto.

Meena Patel \, a pharmacist, becomes Pi's wife after he settles in Canada. They live in Toronto.

Nikhil Patel (Nick) is Pi's son.

Usha Patel is Pi's young daughter.

Pi's Friends and Associates in India:

Satish Kumar (the first of two characters with the same name) is Pi's biology teacher at Petit Séminaire, a secondary school in Pondicherry. He is an atheist, rationalist and an active Communist whose devotion to science inspires Pi to study zoology in college.

Satish Kumar, a poor baker, is a devout Muslim mystic the influence of whose faith leads Pi to study religion at college. (Majoring At the University of Toronto in zoology and religion is a virtually unique combination.)

The Hindu Pandit is an unnamed character who objects strongly when the Hindi Pi begins practicing other religions.

Father Martin is the Catholic priest who introduces Pi to Christianity leading to a conflict with the Muslim Mr. Kumar, and the Hindu pandit as to which religion Pi should practice. Father Martin exemplifies Christ's love to Pi.

On the Lifeboat:
Note that Pi gives two entirely different accounts of his time on the lifeboat. The first is populated by animals and the second by people.

Richard Parker / Pi: Richard Parker is the unlikely name of the three-year-old Royal Bengal tiger from the Pondicherry Zoo with whom Pi shares a lifeboat after the ship in which they are traveling sinks. (The name turns out to be the result of a comic administrative error.) Pi manages to survive by establishing himself as the alpha male while Richard is an omega, submissively accepting Pi's dominance. The tiger represents Pi's instinctive and brutal, animal nature which he must learn to control if he is to be fully human.

The Hyena / The Cook: The Hyena is an ugly, violent animal intent on survival without reference to the survival of others. The Cook is likewise violent and determined to survive. He hoards food on the lifeboat, kills the sailor and Pi's mother, and is finally stabbed to death by Pi.

Orange Juice / Pi's mother: Orange Juice is the name Pi gives to a female orangutan that floats to the lifeboat on a raft of bananas. Eventually, the hyena attacks her, and despite her brave efforts to resist she is killed./ This is the same fate suffered by Pi's mother at the hands of the cook.

The Zebra / the Taiwanese Sailor: The zebra breaks a leg jumping into the lifeboat and becomes the hyena's first victim. The sailor is as beautiful and graceful as the zebra, but he too breaks his leg jumping from the ship. The leg becomes infected and the cook amputates it. Like the zebra, the sailor dies slowly and painfully.

The Blind Frenchman is a castaway whom Pi meets by chance in the middle of the ocean. He is killed by Richard Parker before he can kill Pi.

Members of the Commission of Inquiry:
Tomohiro Okamoto is an official from the Maritime Department of the Japanese Ministry of Transport investigating the sinking of the Japanese ship *Tsimtsum*. He conducts exhaustive interviews in Mexico with Pi while he is recovering from his ordeal.

Atsuro Chiba is Mr. Okamoto's assistant. While his superior is experienced and cynical, he lacks experience in investigating survival stories. He is naïve and trusting.

How to use this study guide:

The questions are not designed to test you but to help you to locate and to understand characters, settings, and themes in the text. They do not normally have simple answers, nor is there always one answer. Consider a range of possibly interpretations - preferably by discussing the questions with others.

Literary terms are in *italics*. These terms are defined towards the end of this guide. An activity is also included to aid in the understanding of these terms.

Analysis of the novel

Author's Note

The note creates a *frame story* by using elements of Martel's real life to introduce a fiction (note that the book's subtitle is "A NOVEL" in capital letters). In doing this, the author is deliberately obscuring the boundary between fact and fiction - what actually happened and what happened only in the writer's imagination.

The BestNotes author helpfully states that the Indian setting is authentic, "The formerly French territory in south India where Pondicherry is located, of course, exists. Even the coffee house in Pondicherry exists, across the road from the Trivandrum Zoo. The "Pondicherry Zoo" does not exist, but the Botanical Gardens do." The final paragraph, a rather conventional list of the people the author would like to thank, is actually a delightful mixture of the real (e.g. "Mr. Moacyr Scilar ... the Canadian Council for the Arts") and the fictional ("Mr. Patel ... three officials of exemplary professionalism").

1. The author defines fiction as "the selective transforming of reality ... The twisting of it to bring out its essence" (viii). Relate that statement to any novel which you know well and like. In what way does that writer transform reality in order to bring out its essence?

2. In direct contrast to the above statement, most of the Note is used to establish that the story really happened and that the writer tried his best to give an accurate account of it ("any inaccuracies or mistakes are mine" [xii]). How does the author seek to convince the reader of factual realism of the story?

3. The Wikipedia entry describes this as "a fantasy adventure novel." Why do you think that the writer begins by insisting that he is writing realistic fiction?

4. The opening sentence of the book reads, "This book was born as I was hungry" (vii). The author then tells us that he went to India because "I had a little money," and we also learn that in Pondicherry he met an elderly man, Mr. Francis Adirubasamy, who told him of Pi's story in "the Indian Coffee House" where "[t]he coffee is goo and they serve French toast" (viii). Thus, the author is not talking about physical hunger. What kinds of "hunger" do you think he has in mind? (***Note:*** Although the 'author-*narrator*' in the novel is not Yann Martel, you may want to read Martel's own account of the origin of the novel which you can find in the essay "How I Wrote *Life of Pi*." It is available on-line. See Works Cited.)

5. The idea that one is about to read "a story to make you believe in God" is a great 'hook' (xi). However, by this statement the author does set the bar pretty high. At the end of the novel you will have to decide for yourself whether this statement is true for the characters and for you as reader.

PART ONE: Toronto and Pondicherry

Chapter 1

The narrative is (as the author said it would be in the Note) in the first person. It seems to be *stream of consciousness* writing, that is, ideas flood out onto the page with no obvious pattern of organization and with many apparent digressions. One idea leads to another idea, the connections apparently being purely subjective. The result is confusion, and an intriguing, jumble of ideas. Of course, the flow of ideas is not random at all; it is carefully controlled by the author. Everything fits with everything else, but this is only evident at the end of the novel.

The *narrator* (Pi) says that for his Bachelor's degree, "[m]y majors were religious studies and zoology" (3). This is a strange combination of theology and science which will run throughout the book. The subjects of his theses are significant for our understanding of Pi's character. The "thyroid gland of the three-toed sloth" sounds dryly scientific, but Pi selected the sloth because of it "lives a peaceful, vegetarian life in perfect harmony with its environment" (4). This might also describe Pi's aim in life. The cosmogony theories of the sixteenth-century Kabbalist Isaac Luria are unlikely to be familiar to most readers. (Miriam Webster defines 'cosmogony' as "**1.**a theory of the origin of the universe; 2. the creation or origin of the world or universe.") At the very least, however, we understand that for Pi (and also for Martel) questions of faith in God and respect for scientific knowledge are complementary rather than (as they are more normally seen) mutually exclusive.

[***Note 1:*** The SparkNotes author has a more detailed explanation of Luria's theory of the creation of the universe and its relevance to the novel. ***Note 2***: That a book which explores complex philosophical ideas should have won so many awards is hardly surprising, but that it should have become an international bestseller (well over ten million sold) is both surprising and reassuring. There is still, it appears, an audience for demanding reading.]

6. What does the opening sentence of the novel suggest about the story which the novel will tell?

7. Why is the *narrator* (Pi) attracted to sloths?

8. What is the speaker's attitude to agnostics? Explain the statement, "muddled agnostics who didn't know which way was up, who were in the thrall of reason, that fool's gold for the bright." In what way do agnostics remind him of sloths? Why is this connection *ironic*? (Note that Pi respects both believers and atheists because he admires those who have a firm commitment to some belief.)

9. Although it may not appear so, the reader actually gets a lot of information about the speaker's story (e.g. the name of at least one character, the starting and ending points of the story, the suffering he underwent, etc.). Make a list of the facts you can gather.

10. The speaker is by nature and by experience sensitive to others. He uses physical *images* to describe his psychological suffering. Thus when Richard Parker abandons him, he writes, "that pain is like an axe that chops at my heart" (6). Also, when the waiter criticizes him for eating with his hands, he writes, "He had no idea how deeply those words wounded me. They were like nails being driven into my flesh" (7). Anything you can add on those two *similes*?

Pi includes his 'bucket list' of cities he would like to visit. They are: Mecca, Islam's holiest city; Varanasi, holiest city of Hindus; Jerusalem, holiest city of Jews and Christians; Paris, the city of magnificent swimming pools (according to Mamaji), and Oxford, a center of academic excellence.

Chapter 2

A short chapter! Raises two questions: Who is "He," and why is the chapter in italics (7). The answer to the second question is that the Author's Note was also in italics, so the voice we hear is that of the author. That means that "He" must be the adult Pi from whom the author got his story.

Chapter 3

This chapter explains how the ***narrator*** came to be named after a swimming pool.

11. In what ways is Mamaji's passion for swimming pools similar to the *narrator*'s interest in sloths?

Chapter 4.

12. What are the arguments against keeping animals in zoos which the ***narrator*** mentions? For each objection, what is his counter-argument

13. The *narrator* links the subjects of zoos and religions. At the start of the discussion, he writes, "I have heard nearly as much nonsense about zoos as I have heard about God and religion" (15). At the end of the discussion, he writes, "I know zoos are no longer in people's good graces. Religion faces the same problem. Certain illusions about freedom plague them both" (19). Now this is pretty deep theology, and therefore not easy. **The *narrator*** has explained how the illusion of freedom applies to animals (i.e. animals in the wild are not actually free because they are tied to their territory without which their lives would be meaningless and terrifying), but how do you think that the illusion of freedom applies to religion?

Chapter 5

This chapter is about how Piscine Molitor Patel renamed himself (like so many other religious thinkers did) Pi Patel.

14. To what religious figure does the *narrator* compare himself at the time when he developed his plan to change his name?

Chapter 6

15. How do you think that the detail that Pi's kitchen cabinets are *"jam-packed"* might relate to his story (25)?

Chapter 7

16. Mr. Satish Kumar, Pi's biology teacher, is described as "the first avowed atheist I ever met" (25). What do you notice about the physical description of Mr. Kumar? What in his own life has led Mr. Kumar to this philosophy? How does he defend his belief that "'Religion is darkness'" (27)?

17. Pi admires atheists because "[l]ike me, they go as far as the legs of reason will carry them - and then they leap" (28). Explain how this applies to, first, religious people (like Pi) and to atheists (like Mr. Kumar). Why does Pi not respect agnostics?

18. Mr. Satish Kumar is also described as "an active Communist" (25). Where does he express his communist views in this chapter?

Chapter 8

The chapter begins with a list of the consciously, and occasionally unconsciously, cruel and harmful things that people do to animals in zoos.

19. Pi says that "the was another animal even more dangerous than us, and one that was extremely common too … the animal as seen through human eyes" (31). Explain what he means by this.

20. Explain what Pi means when he writes, "The obsession with putting ourselves at the center of everything is the bane not only of theologians but also of zoologists" (31).

21. Why does Pi's father use such an extreme demonstration to bring home to Pi and Ravi that "an animal is an animal" (31).

Chapter 9

This chapter describes the distances that different species of animals will allow a human to approach before they seek to get away. This will be significant in the story later.

Chapter 10

22. What is it in animal psychology which naturally discourages them from wanting to escape from their compounds in a zoo? What reasons are sufficient to overcome this natural aversion and prompt animals to escape?

Chapter 11

This chapter illustrates the fact that even escaped animals are "simply wild creatures seeking to fit in" (42).

23. Explain the last three lines of this chapter.

Chapter 12
24. Why is Pi so anxious to tell his story? What is implied by the following description of Pi, "Memory is an ocean and he bobs on its surface" (42)?

Chapter 13.
25. Explain the psychology used by the circus animal trainer to subdue the animals to his will.
[Note that many of the points made in this chapter will be significant later.]

Chapter 14
26. What is characteristic about the "omega animal" in every group (44)?
Chapter 15
27. What three religions are represented by the things that make Pi's house "a temple" (45)?

Chapter 16:
    Pi explains that his first introduction to God was through the Hindu religion. He says that he remains a Hindu because, "The universe makes sense to me through Hindu eyes ... With its notions in mind I see my place in the universe" (48-9).

28. What does Pi mean by his assertion that we are all "in limbo, without religion, until some figure introduces us to God"?
29. The chapter ends with the assertion that Hinduism, Islam and Christianity share certain essential truths. What evidence from world history would you use to prove that this is certainly a minority view over the last two thousand years? Is it a view with which you would agree or disagree?

Chapter 17:
30. Pi explains his 'conversion' to Christianity by a Father Martin, Catholic priest. Pi calls him "that troublesome rabbi" (56). Why?
31. Pi is at first repulsed by the whole idea of Christ's suffering and dying on the cross. It is entirely alien to his conception of what a god should be. What is it that finally attracts Pi to this new faith?

Chapter 18-20:
    Pi explains his 'conversion' to Islam under the guidance of Mr. Kumar the bread-maker (who co-incidentally has the same name as Pi's Communist, atheist biology teacher). At first, he finds Islamic prayer rather strange. He describes it humorously as "nothing but an easy form of exercise ... Hot-weather yoga for the Bedouins" (60).
    The BestNotes author informs us, "There is also a real-life Satish Kumar. He is a former Jain monk from India who literally walked across the world to promote disarmament and raise awareness of the beauty and connectedness of all

things. His book, *Path Without Destination*, describes his journey and his beliefs and makes him a likely inspiration for the characters of Mr. and Mr. Kumar."

32. What is it that attracts Pi to Islam?

33. Pi describes two experiences where he feels the "presence of God" (62). What do they have in common? What does the sentence "Atman met Allah" mean (62)?

Chapter 21-2:

These chapters explain the limits of reason and the leap to faith. Agnostics, who explain the human mind as they would a light bulb, miss "the better story": in the universe in which we live, there is "an alignment ... along moral lines," love is "the founding principle of existence," and reason come to the end of its ability to understand can have "a trusting sense of presence and of ultimate purpose" (63).

34. These chapters are very short, yet the author has said that they are at the core of the novel. Why?

Chapter 23:

Pi describes what he *ironically* calls his "introduction to interfaith dialogue" (70). It's quite a *comic* chapter, starting with the implausible meeting of all three of Pi's spiritual mentors with his parents and then their silly bickering that 'my religion's better than your religion.' It seems that, just as animals in the zoo just want a place to call their own where they feel in control, so people use religion to make their lives more comfortable because without it life is pretty terrifying. Pi and the author seem to be indicating that religion should be something more than this.

35. What is it that Pi says which silences all debate and why is what he says completely unanswerable?

Chapter 24-8:

Pi has to face the barbed humor of his brother, the opposition of those in each of his three religions who believe that their religion is exclusive of all others, and the incomprehension of his parents who regard religion as a thing of the past in Modern India. Despite the opposition, Pi persuades his parents to buy him a prayer mat and to allow him to become baptized into the Christian faith. Notice how powerful it is when Pi quotes Mahatma Gandhi in support of his views.

36. What is significant about the coral tree which grows near the spot that Pi selects for his prayers? (How does it embody his view of religion?)

Chapter 29:

The political situation of the mid-1970s described in this chapter is historically accurate. Prime Minister Indira Gandhi imprisoned her political enemies, censored the press, and disregarded constitutional rights. Her opponents claimed that she did irreparable harm to the Indian democracy, although a supporter of Mrs. Gandhi would, of course, have a different view.

37. Earlier Pi explained that zoo animals seldom attempt to escape from their designated areas and even when they do they find the closest place where they feel secure. In what ways is the movement of the Patel family like and in what ways unlike the behavior of zoo animals?

Chapter 30:
Pi's house, and his life, is much more than "a box full of [religious] icons." Religion is the basis for a full life, not an alternative to living in the real world.

Chapter 31:
38. The two Mr. Kumars happen to meet at the zoo (another unlikely coincidence). Explain the dialogue which closes the chapter:
"'This one's a Grant's zebra,' I said.
Mr. Kumar said, '*Equus burchelli boemi.*'
Mr. Kumar said, '*Allahu akbar.*'
I said, 'It's very pretty.'"

Chapter 32:
39. What is zoomorphism? Why do animals sometimes adopt animals of another species?

Chapter 33:
There is a tantalizingly vague reference in the chapter to Richard Parker. The reader is being manipulated!

Chapter 34-5:
40. Why must you "take life the way it comes at you and make the best of it" (91)?

Chapter 36:
This is the last chapter in which the author-*narrator* will speak directly to the reader in his own voice until the beginning of Part Three when the *narrator* continues the story from a point where Pi himself feels that the story is complete.

41. Why do you think that the author ends Part One with the assurance, "*This story has a happy ending*"?

PART TWO: The Pacific Ocean

Chapter 37:

The BestNotes author informs us that *Tsimtsum* means "contraction" or "withdrawal," and speculates that it "may mean that God has withdrawn from Pi to make room for Pi to develop as an independent creature ..." Finally the reader discovers the identity of Richard Parker: having spent most of the chapter encouraging Richard to swim towards the lifeboat, Pi realizes the implications of sharing his lifeboat with a three-year-old Bengal tiger. Pi reminds the reader of his father's demonstration involving a tiger and a goat!

42. What elements of the description of the shipwreck and its immediate aftermath strike you as not being realistic?

43. Faced with the inexplicable loss of everything, Pi asks rhetorically "what is the purpose of reason ... Why can't reason give greater answers?" (98). Based on Part One, what can give greater answers? Explain.

Chapter 38-9:

44. The narrative goes back to give the context of the disaster. In many ways, this description appears to be a more realistic account of how the ship began to sink. There are, however, still aspects of the description which are unrealistic. What are they?

Chapter 40-2:

Pi says, "Had I considered my prospects in light of reason, I surely would have given up and let go of the oar, hoping that I might drown before being eaten." Something, however, gives Pi the determination and will to survive. He says, "I held on to the oar, I just held on, God knows why." When reason reaches its limit... thus he takes his situation "one terror at a time, Pacific before tiger" (107).

The account of the arrival of the orangutan once again strains credibility.

45. The color orange predominates in this chapter. Orange is a color with particular connotations for Hindus. What are they and how do they relate to Pi's situation?

46. Explain why Pi welcomes the creature as "the Virgin Mary ... '... blessed Great Mother, Pondicherry fertility goddess ...'" (111).

Chapter 43-5:

The SparkNotes author comments on what Pi is about to experience in the lifeboat, "Pi's true education in nature's savagery begins in this gruesome section." It is true that as a child his father, Mr. Patel, did his best to teach Ravi and Pi about the nature of wild animals and the danger of forgetting it, but only now does Pi truly come to understand what his father was trying to tell him.

47. What did Pi find surprising about his reaction to the plight of the zebra which had had its leg bitten off by the hyena?

48. Why does Pi find "the ecosystem on this lifeboat … decidedly baffling" (122)?

Chapter 46:
The description of the hyena's attack on the zebra is graphic and horrifying.

49. What two things in this chapter bring home to Pi the reality that his family is dead and that he is alone?

Chapter 47:
50. In this chapter, Pi underestimates two things. What are they? How does the lesson he learns relate to his own survival?

51. Explain exactly why, "An adult female orangutan cannot defeat an adult male spotted hyena" (130).

52. Why do you think that Pi describes the dead orangutan as "like a simian Christ on the Cross" (132)? ['simian': "of, relating to, or resembling monkeys or apes" (Merriam-Webster).]

Chapter 48-9:
53. What do the stories of the capture of Richard Parker and Pi's struggle to survive show them to have in common?

Chapter 50-2:
54. When he finds the water and emergency rations Pi's desire to survive overcomes one of his cultural practices. Explain how this uncharacteristic action mirrors something he has earlier noticed in the orangutan.

55. Comment on the final item of survival stores which Pi lists.

Chapter 53-5:
In one of the most detailed sections so far, Pi describes his efforts to stay alive. His faith gives him the determination to live, "I will not die. I refuse it …so long as God is with me, I will not die. Amen" (148). The account of the construction of the raft makes it sound plausible, but anyone who has ever tried to make a raft will know how difficult it would actually be. Two deaths occur: the hyena and the rat.

Chapter 56-7:
In these chapters, Pi progresses from six unrealistic plans to kill Richard Parker to one ambitious plan to keep him alive. He is able to do this because he is able to overcome his fear of the tiger, and "fear is life's only true opponent. Only fear can defeat life" (161).

56. What is the *Prusten*? How does it completely change the way Pi regards his relationship with the tiger?

57. How does Pi feel that Richard Parker "pushed me to go on living" (164)?
The SparkNotes author argues that one point the author is making in the novel is that "animals and humans aren't such different creatures after all." In support of this, he/she cites the fact that the tiger has a human name and that Pi's name suggests the word *pisces,* or *fish.*

Chapter 58-9:

Only when he is not engaged in the practical activity of keeping himself alive does Pi give way to despair, as when he is suddenly struck by the immensity of the Pacific Ocean and thinks, "There was so much water. And I was all alone. All alone ... My situation was patently hopeless" (169).

Chapter 60-2:

58. What difference does Pi note between the way he feels about his suffering at night and during the day?
59. Pi writes that, "A lifetime of peaceful vegetarianism stood between me and the willful beheading of a fish" (183). How does he overcome his inhibitions? How is this development another indication that men and animals are not so very different?
60. In what ways is existence in the lifeboat "with every passing day ... resembling a zoo enclosure more and more" (188-9).
61. The BestNotes author states, "The Hindu saint, Markandeya, has more in common with Pi than Pi describes." Research this commonality.

Chapter 63-5

The length of Pi's survival, when placed against real people, indicates the improbability of the story on the realistic level. The schedule which Pi produces has one constant element: prayers. However, his faith is being tested. The salt-water boils reminds one of the suffering of Job, "So went Satan forth from the presence of the LORD, and smote Job with sore boils from the sole of his foot unto his crown" (King James Bible, Job 2:7).

Pi writes about his failure to understand the navigation section of the survival manual. As a result of this, and the fact that he had no means to control the lifeboat, he drifted. Comment on the symbolic significance of the statement, "Time became distance for me in the way in which it is for mortals - I travelled down the road of life ... I found out later that I travelled a narrow road, the Pacific equatorial counter-current" (193-4).

Chapter 66-70

These chapters focus on his fishing. What makes Pi comment of himself, "I descended to a level of savagery I never imagined possible" (197). "Hanuman refers to the Hindu god with a simian form. He is a symbol of physical strength, perseverance, and devotion. He helps when faced with ordeals or challenges" (BestNotes).

62. Sea-life gravitates to the raft. Pi comments, "What I saw was an upside-down town, small, quiet and peaceable, whose citizens went about with the sweet civility of angels. The sight was a welcome relief for my frayed nerves" (198). Why does Pi find this sight so calming?

63. How does Pi's experience of butchering the turtle lead him to conclude, "It was time to impose myself and carve out my territory?

Chapter 71-2:
These two chapters deal respectively with the theory and practice of tiger taming. The first is composed like an instruction manual, and the second deals with the reality.

64. Comment on the **ironic** humor of the chapter opening, "To those who should ever find themselves in a predicament such as I was in ..." (202).

65. Pi realizes that "Richard Parker did not really want to attack me. Tigers, indeed all animals, do not favor violence as a means of settling scores" (206). Explain why this is.

Chapter 73-7:
Despite his best efforts, Pi begins to deteriorate intellectually (he longs for a book), spiritually (he swings like a pendulum between faith and despair), and physically.

66. There is quite a lot about bodily functions in these chapters, particularly related to Richard Parker's feces: cleaning them up, using possession of them as a sign of mastery, and even attempting to eat them! Why do you think that the author makes these details so graphic? (Martel himself commented, "I live in a society that is in terrified denial of 'unpalatable' realities, realities I prefer to face" (Renton).

Chapter 78-79
67. Pi says of life on a lifeboat, "You must make adjustments if you want to survive" (217), and later "You can get used to anything ..." (222-3). How is this illustrated by Richard Parker's epic battle with the mako shark?

Chapter 80-84:
Pi (formerly a vegetarian) becomes entirely "indiscriminate" about what he eats (225). This is backed up by some pretty stomach-churning descriptions of what he actually does eat and how he eats it. Finally, it seems to him that he has been reduced to the level of an animal, "It came as an unmistakable indication to me of how low I had sunk ... I ate like an animal ... exactly the way Richard Parker ate" (225).

Chapter 85-9:
68. Compare and contrast the reactions of Pi and of Richard Parker to the lightning and to the near miss with the oil tanker. How do these encounters

emphasize the essential difference between men and animals?
69. Pi makes three desperate (and ultimately unsuccessful) attempts to communicate his predicament in this section. What are they? What is the one attempt at communication which might be seen as, to some extent, successful?

Chapter 90-1:
The blindness which Richard Parker and Pi both suffer appears real enough. It could also be seen as a symbol for Pi's loss of faith and humanity as his physical condition continues to deteriorate. Pi's encounter with another blind person adrift in a boat is also presented as though it actually happened, but it must be a hallucination.

70. What do you think that the other survivor represents? Explain your answer.

Chapter 92:
Pi prefaces his description of the floating island with the *ironic* comment that "there will be many who disbelieve the following episode" (256).

71. The color green and the lote tree have important connotations in Islam. What are they and how do they relate to Pi's current situation?
72. The SparkNotes author comments of this part of the story, "The floating island symbolizes Pi's own despair ... The carnivorous vegetation represents Pi's pessimism, his dwindling hope that he will ever be found. To stay on the island would be to give up." How convincing do you find this explanation?

Chapter 93:
73. What does Pi find so disappointing at the way in which his relationship with Richard Parker ends?

Chapter 94:
74. Pi describes how "a member of my own species found me" (285). Explain his rather odd choice of words here.

Pi describes the beach as "like the cheek of God, and somewhere two eyes were glittering with pleasure and a mouth was smiling at having [Pi] there" (285). It seems that he has found his faith again.

PART THREE: Benito Juárez Infirmary, Tomatlán, Mexico

Chapter 95:
75. The narrative voice switches from Pi to the author. With the change realism appears to reassert itself. What details in the chapter imply that the narrative has returned to documentary realism from the subjectivity of Pi's account?

Chapter 96-100:
76. In this section the investigators, Mr. Okamoto and Mr. Chiba, are presented as *comic* figures. How is this done? Why is this done?

77. Mr. Chiba notes without understanding that Pi stashes cookies under his bed sheet. Why does Pi do this?

78. Mr. Okamoto and Mr. Chiba tell Pi that they do not believe his survival story. Make a list of the improbabilities which they find in it.

79. Explain what Pi means when he says, "'be excessively reasonable and you risk throwing out the universe with the bathwater'" (298).

80. Pi argues that, "'Isn't telling about something - using words ... already something of an invention? Isn't just looking upon this world already something of an invention? (302). Neither Mr. Okamoto nor Mr. Chiba understands what Pi means. What does he mean?

81. Pi tells "'another story'" (303). After hearing it, Mr. Okamoto realizes that, "'His stories match,'" and that "'he's the tiger'" (311). What new light does this identification case on Pi's earlier statement, "[W]ithout Richard Parker, I wouldn't be alive today to tell you my story" (164), and on Pi's efforts to train Richard Parker?

82. Produce a graphic to show the matching of the two stories.

83. Just before they leave, Pi asks Mr. Okamoto and Mr. Chiba which of the two stories he has told they prefer and they agree that they prefer "dry, yeastless factuality," or the one with animals. Pi comments, "'And so it goes with God'" (317). What do you think that he means? How does it relate to the claim that this is a story that will make you "believe in God" (x)? Did it?

84. What is significant about the last sentence of Mr. Okamoto's report?

85. The first part of the novel starts twenty years after Pi's ordeal at sea and ends with the author's assurance, *"This story has a happy ending"* (93). Why does the author think so? Do you agree that the ending is *"happy"*?

Post-reading Activities

1. The Origins of the Novel

Here is the account of where Martel got idea for this novel according to GradeSaver:

> Yann Martel was perusing through John Updike's rather negative review of *Max and the Cats*, a story about a Jewish family who run a zoo in Germany during the years leading up to the Holocaust. They decide to leave Germany, but the boat they take sinks, and only one member of the family survives, ending up on a lifeboat with a black panther ... Years later, while in India, without a story he believed in or much hope, he suddenly remembered this premise, and the rest of *Life of Pi* came to him.

Here is the version of which appears in SparkNotes:

> In a 2002 interview ... Martel discusses reading an unfavorable review of Scliar's novel [*Max and the Cats*, 1981] in the *New York Times Book Review* penned by John Updike and, despite Updike's disparagement, being entranced by the premise. As was later reported, no such review existed, and John Updike himself claimed no knowledge of Scliar's novel ... Martel claims never to have read *Max and the Cats* before beginning to write *Life of Pi*. He has since blamed his faulty memory for the ... gaffe and has declined further discussion on the topic.

You can read Martel's account in "How I Wrote *Life of Pi*" which is available on-line. What is the truth? How does the truth affect your appreciation of the novel?

2. An Interview

Chapter 16 (in particular) asserts the syncretism, or union, of the principals of the three major religions: Hinduism, Islam and Christianity. If you are a member of a religious community, conduct an interview with your priest, imam, rabbi, etc. Get their reaction to what Pi is saying. Write up the interview as a magazine of webpage article.

Works Cited

Cassie, Donna L. "TheBestNotes on *Life of Pi*". *TheBestNotes.com.* 12 May 2008 Web. 13 July 2013.

Cullina, Alice. Chazelle, Damien ed. "*Life of Pi* Study Guide". GradeSaver, 30 November 2008 Web. 13 July 2013.

Martel, Yann. "How I Wrote *Life of Pi.*" *Let's Talk Books.* Powell's Books. Web. 19 Jul 2013.

Renton, Jennie. "Yann Martel Interview." *Textualities.* Main Point Books, 2005. Web. 19 Jul 2013.

SparkNotes Editors. "SparkNote on Life of Pi." SparkNotes.com. SparkNotes LLC. 2006. 28 Jun. 2013. Web. 13 July 2013.

Graphic organizer: Plot

Plot graph for *Life of Pi*

CLIMAX

RESOLUTION

FALLING ACTION
DENOUEMENT

RISING ACTION
CONFLICT

EXPOSITION

Activity: Literary terms

As you use each term in the study guide, fill in the definition of the term and include an example from the text to show how it is used. The first definition is supplied. Find an example in the text to complete it.

Term: frame-story
Definition: *a story within which the main narrative is placed*
Example:

****

Term: genre
Definition:
Example:

****

Term: image
Definition:
Example:

****

Term: ironic, ironically
Definition:
Example:

****

Term: narrator
Definition:
Example:

****

Term: simile
Definition:
Example:

****

Literary terms

NOTE: Not all of these terms may be relevant to this particular text.

Adjective: part of speech- a word that describes a noun (e.g. the <u>thin</u> man)

Ambiguous, ambiguity: when a statement is unclear in meaning- ambiguity may be deliberate or accidental

Analogy: a comparison which treats two things as identical in one or more specified ways

Climax: the conflict to which the action has been building since the start of the play or story.

Comic hyperbole: deliberately inflated, extravagant language used for comic effect

Comic Inversion: reversing the normal order of things for comic effect

Connotation: the ideas, feelings and associations generated by a word or phrase

Dark comedy: comedy which has a serious implication

Dialogue: a conversation between two or more people in direct speech

Diction: the writer's choice of words in order to create a particular effect

Euphemism: a polite word for an ugly truth for example, a person is said to be sleeping when they are actually dead

Equivocation: saying something which is capable of two interpretations with the intention of misrepresenting the truth

Fallacy: a misconception resulting from incorrect reasoning

Foreshadow: a statement or action which gives the reader a hint of what is likely to happen later in the narrative

Frame narrative: a story within which the main narrative is placed

Genre: the type of literature into which a particular text falls (e.g. drama, poetry, novel)

Hubris: pride- in Greek tragedy it is the hero's belief that he can challenge the will of the gods.

Image, imagery: figurative language such as simile, metaphor, personification etc., or a description which conjures u a particularly vivid picture

Imply, implication: when the text suggests to the reader a meaning which it does not actually state

Infer, inference: the reader's act of going beyond what is stated in the text to draw conclusions

Irony, ironic: a form of humor which undercuts the apparent meaning

    Dramatic irony: when an action has a significance that is obvious to the reader but not to one or more of the characters

    Tragic irony: when a character says (or does) something which will have a serious, even fatal, consequence for him/ her. The audience is aware of the error, but the character is not.

Verbal irony: the conscious use of particular words which are appropriate to what is being said

Juxtaposition: literally putting two things side by side for purposes of comparison and/ or contrast

Literal: the surface level of a statement

Malapropism: the unconscious misuse of language by a character so that key words are replaced by similar sounding words, which make no sense in the context in which they are used, the effect being unintentionally comic

Metaphor, metaphorical: the description of one thing by direct comparison with another (e.g. the coal-black night)

Extended metaphor: a comparison which is developed at length

Melodramatic: action and/or dialogue that is inflated or extravagant- frequently used for comic effect

Motif: a frequently repeated idea, image or situation

Motivation: why a character acts as he/ she does- in modern literature motivation is seen as psychological

Narrates, narrator: the voice that the reader hears in the text

Oxymoron: the juxtaposition of two terms normally thought of as opposite (e.g. the silent scream)

Parable: a story with a moral lesson (e.g. the Good Samaritan)

Paradox, paradoxical: a statement or situation which appears self-contradictory and therefore absurd

Pathos: is pity, or rather the ability of a text to make the audience or reader feel pity

Personified, personification: a simile or metaphor in which an inanimate object or abstract idea is described by comparison with a human

Plot: a chain of events linked by cause and effect

Pun: a deliberate play on words where a particular word has two or more meanings both appropriate in some way to what is being said

Realism: a text that describes the action in a way that appears to reflect life

Rhetoric: the art of public speaking and more specifically the techniques which make speaking and writing effective

Rhyming couplets: two consecutive lines of poetry ending in a full rhyme

Rhythm: literally the 'musical beat' of the words. In good writing, the rhythm of the words is clearly appropriate to what the words describe, so the rhythm is a part of the total meaning of the words

Role: means function- characters in plays (particularly minor characters) frequently have specific functions

Sarcasm: stronger than irony - it involves a deliberate attack on a person or idea with the intention of mocking

Setting: the environment in which the narrative (or part of the narrative) takes place

Simile: a description of one thing by explicit comparison with another (e.g. my love is like a red, red rose)

   Extended simile: a comparison which is developed at length

Soliloquy: where a character in a play, normally alone on the stage, directly addresses the audience. By convention, a character is truthful in a soliloquy, though they may, of course be wrong or self-deceiving

Style: the way in which a writer chooses to express him/ herself. Style is a vital aspect of meaning since how something is expressed can crucially affect what is being written or spoken

Suspense: the building of tension in the reader

Symbol, symbolic, symbolism, symbolize: a physical object which comes to represent an abstract idea (e.g. the sun may symbolize life)

Themes: important concepts, beliefs and ideas explored and presented in a text

Tone: literally the sound of a text - How words sound (either in the mouth of an actor or the head of a reader) can crucially affect meaning

Tragic: King Richard III and Macbeth are both murderous tyrants, yet only Macbeth is a *tragic* figure. Why? Because Macbeth has the potential to be great, recognizes the error he has made and all that he has lost in making it, and dies bravely in a way that seems to accept the justice of the punishment.

Classroom Use of Study Guide questions

Although there are both closed and open questions in the Study Guide, very few of them have simple, right or wrong answers. They are designed to encourage in-depth discussion, disagreement, and (eventually) consensus. Above all, they aim to encourage students to go to the text to support their conclusions and interpretations.

I am not so arrogant as to presume to tell teachers how they should use this resource. I used it in the following ways, each of which ensured that students were well prepared for class discussion and presentations.

1. Set a reading assignment for the class and tell everyone to be aware that the questions will be the focus of whole class discussion the next class.

2. Set a reading assignment for the class and allocate particular questions to sections of the class (e.g. if there are four questions, divide the class into four sections, etc.).

In class, form discussion groups containing one person who has prepared each question and allow time for feedback within the groups.

Have feedback to the whole class on each question by picking a group at random to present their answers and to follow up with class discussion.

3. Set a reading assignment for the class, but do not allocate questions.

In class, divide students into groups and allocate to each group one of the questions related to the reading assignment the answer to which they will have to present formally to the class.

Allow time for discussion and preparation.

4. Set a reading assignment for the class, but do not allocate questions.

In class, divide students into groups and allocate to each group one of the questions related to the reading assignment.

Allow time for discussion and preparation.

Now reconfigure the groups so that each group contains at least one person who has prepared each question and allow time for feedback within the groups.

5. Before starting to read the text, allocate specific questions to individuals or pairs. (It is best not to allocate all questions to allow for other approaches and variety. One in three questions or one in four seems about right.) Tell students that they will be leading the class discussion on their question. They will need to start with a brief presentation of the issues and then conduct a question and answer session. After this, they will be expected to present a brief review of the discussion.

6. Having finished the text, arrange the class into groups of 3, 4 or 5. Tell each group to select as many questions from the Study Guide as there are members of the group.

Each individual is responsible for drafting out a written answer to one question, and each answer should be a substantial paragraph.

To the Reader
Ray strives to make his products the best that they can be. If you have any comments or questions about this book *please* contact the author through his email: **moore.ray1@yahoo.com**
Visit his website at **http://www.raymooreauthor.com**
Also by Ray Moore: Most books are available from amazon.com as paperbacks and at most online eBook retailers.

Fiction:
The Lyle Thorne Mysteries: each book features five tales from the Golden Age of Detection:
Investigations of The Reverend Lyle Thorne
Further Investigations of The Reverend Lyle Thorne
Early Investigations of Lyle Thorne
Sanditon Investigations of The Reverend Lyle Thorne
Final Investigations of The Reverend Lyle Thorne

Non-fiction:
The ***Critical Introduction series*** is written for high school teachers and students and for college undergraduates. Each volume gives an in-depth analysis of a key text:
"The Stranger" by Albert Camus: A Critical Introduction (Revised Second Edition)
"The General Prologue" by Geoffrey Chaucer: A Critical Introduction
"Pride and Prejudice" by Jane Austen: A Critical Introduction
"The Great Gatsby" by F. Scott Fitzgerald: A Critical Introduction

The Text and Critical Introduction series <u>differs</u> from the Critical introduction series as these books contain the original text and in the case of the medieval texts an interlinear translation to aid the understanding of the text. The commentary allows the reader to develop a deeper understanding of the text and themes within the text.
"Sir Gawain and the Green Knight": Text and Critical Introduction
"The General Prologue" by Geoffrey Chaucer: Text and Critical Introduction
"The Wife of Bath's Prologue and Tale" by Geoffrey Chaucer: Text and Critical Introduction
"Heart of Darkness" by Joseph Conrad: Text and Critical Introduction
"The Sign of Four" by Sir Arthur Conan Doyle Text and Critical Introduction
"A Room with a View" By E.M. Forster: Text and Critical Introduction
"Oedipus Rex" by Sophocles: Text and Critical Introduction

Study guides available in print- listed alphabetically by author
* *denotes also available as an eBook*
"ME and EARL and the Dying GIRL" by Jesse Andrews: A Study Guide

Life of Pi by Yann Martel

"Wuthering Heights" by Emily Brontë: A Study Guide *
"Jane Eyre" by Charlotte Brontë: A Study Guide *
"The Myth of Sisyphus" and "The Stranger" by Albert Camus: Two Study Guides *
"The Meursault Investigation" by Kamel Daoud: A Study Guide
"Great Expectations" by Charles Dickens: A Study Guide *
"The Sign of Four" by Sir Arthur Conan Doyle: A Study Guide *
"A Room with a View" by E. M. Forster: A Study Guide
"Looking for Alaska" by John Green: A Study Guide
"Paper Towns" by John Green: A Study Guide
"Unbroken" by Laura Hillenbrand: A Study Guide
"The Kite Runner" by Khaled Hosseini: A Study Guide
"A Thousand Splendid Suns" by Khaled Hosseini: A Study Guide
"Go Set a Watchman" by Harper Lee: A Study Guide
"On the Road" by Jack Keruoac: A Study Guide
"The Secret Life of Bees" by Sue Monk Kidd: A Study Guide
"An Inspector Calls" by J.B. Priestley: A Study Guide
"The Catcher in the Rye" by J.D. Salinger: A Study Guide
"Macbeth" by William Shakespeare: A Study Guide *
"Othello" by William Shakespeare: A Study Guide *
"Antigone" by Sophocles: A Study Guide *
"Oedipus Rex" by Sophocles: A Study Guide
"Cannery Row" by John Steinbeck: A Study Guide
"East of Eden" by John Steinbeck: A Study Guide
"Of Mice and Men" by John Steinbeck: A Study Guide *

Study Guides available as e-books:
"Heart of Darkness" by Joseph Conrad: A Study Guide
"The Mill on the Floss" by George Eliot: A Study Guide
"Lord of the Flies" by William Golding: A Study Guide
"Catch-22" by Joseph Heller: A Study Guide
"Life of Pi" by Yann Martel: A Study Guide
"Nineteen Eighty-Four by George Orwell: A Study Guide
"Selected Poems" by Sylvia Plath: A Study Guide
"Henry IV Part 2" by William Shakespeare: A Study Guide
"Julius Caesar" by William Shakespeare: A Study Guide
"The Pearl" by John Steinbeck: A Study Guide
"Slaughterhouse-Five" by Kurt Vonnegut: A Study Guide
"The Bridge of San Luis Rey" by Thornton Wilder: A Study Guide

Teacher resources: Ray also publishes many more study guides and other resources for classroom use on the 'Teachers Pay Teachers' website:
http://www.teacherspayteachers.com/Store/Raymond-Moore

Made in the USA
Lexington, KY
17 June 2016